TABLE OF CONTENTS

I0409978

FIGURES

ABBREVIATIONS

ANP	Afghan National Police
ANSF	Afghan National Security Forces
ASFF	Afghanistan Security Forces Fund
C-JTSCC	U.S. Central Command Joint Theater Support Contracting Command
CSTC-A	Combined Security Transition Command-Afghanistan
DOD	Department of Defense
FAR	Federal Acquisition Regulation
MOI	Ministry of Interior
PHQ	Provincial Police Headquarters
SIGAR	Special Inspector General for Afghanistan Reconstruction

The Combined Security Transition Command-Afghanistan (CSTC-A)[1] equips and trains the Afghan National Security Forces (ANSF), which includes the Afghan National Police (ANP) and Afghan National Army.[2] CSTC-A uses the Afghanistan Security Forces Fund (ASFF) to provide the ANSF with equipment, supplies, and training, as well as facility and infrastructure repair, renovation, and construction. A portion of the ASFF has been used to purchase fuel for the ANSF.[3]

To purchase fuel for the ANSF, CSTC-A uses blanket purchase agreements[4] issued by the U.S. Central Command Joint Theater Support Contracting Command (C-JTSCC). C-JTSCC executes and oversees contracts and exercises command and control over all contingency contracting forces operating in Afghanistan. Under the blanket purchase agreements, C-JTSCC is the contracting officer organization responsible for administering fuel contracts and CSTC-A provides the contracting officer representative responsible for the ordering and accounting of fuel purchased for the ANSF.

In January 2013, we reported on fuel purchases for the Afghan National Army, which is under the Afghan Ministry of Defense.[5] That report identified weaknesses with CSTC-A's processes governing the ordering, receipt, and payment for fuel used to support vehicles, generators, and power plants. We also found that CSTC-A budget requests for Afghan National Army fuel were potentially overstated because they were based on unsupported data and that CSTC-A planned to provide $1 billion in direct contributions to the Ministry of Defense despite known risks. SIGAR made six recommendations to improve accountability and transparency of funds and fuel; CSTC-A concurred with all the recommendations.

We initiated this audit to evaluate U.S. oversight of fuel purchases for ANP, which is under the Ministry of Interior (MOI). Specifically, this audit assesses:

- the extent to which C-JTSCC and CSTC-A provided oversight of ANP fuel purchases, deliveries, and consumption;
- CSTC-A's efforts to provide direct contributions to the Afghan government to support ANP's logistics transition; and
- the basis and support for CSTC-A's funding request for fiscal year 2013 and its estimates from fiscal years 2014 through 2018.

To accomplish our objectives, we reviewed U.S. regulations and standards, MOI logistics policy, CSTC-A fuel data, Regional Command Southwest[6] fuel data, and U.S. budget data (obligations and disbursements); we also interviewed officials at CSTC-A, C-JTSCC, Regional Command Southwest, MOI's logistics department,[7] Defense Finance and Accounting Services and CSTC-A's local national contractors. We conducted our work in Kabul,

---

[1] CSTC-A responsible is for managing the use of the Afghanistan Security Forces Fund resources, training and equipping ANSF forces, and building the capacity of the Afghan Ministries of Interior and Defense.

[2] The Afghan National Police serves as the single law enforcement agency for Afghanistan, which includes the Afghan Uniformed Police, Afghan Border Police, Afghan National Civil Order Police, and other uniformed enablers (including intelligence, anti-crime, counter narcotics, traffic, medical, and fire).

[3] CSTC-A and C-JTSCC refer to fuel as "petroleum, oils and lubricants" or "POL". We use "fuel" to describe POL throughout the report. Some forms, regulations and agency comments will still refer to "POL".

[4] A blanket purchase agreement is a simplified method of filling requirements that may be needed on an ongoing basis.

[5] Special Inspector General for Afghanistan Reconstruction. *Afghan National Army: Controls Over Fuel for Vehicles, Generators, and Power Plants Need Strengthening to Prevent Fraud, Waste, and Abuse,* Washington, D.C.: 2013.

[6] The Regional Command Southwest is a subordinate command to the International Security Assistance Force; its mission is to conduct counterinsurgency operations in partnership with the Afghan government in order to develop the ANSF and improve governance and economic development. The areas of responsibility include Helmand and Nimroz provinces.

[7] Known as the Material Management Center-Police, the logistics headquarters is housed under the MOI's general logistics department. The MOI logistics department performs control functions for the movement of equipment and material within MOI.

Afghanistan from September 2012 to September 2013, in accordance with generally accepted government auditing standards. A more detailed discussion of our scope and methodology is in appendix I.

BACKGROUND

Since 2005, Congress has appropriated almost $52.8 billion to the ASFF to train, equip and sustain the ANSF, which includes the ANP and the Afghan National Army. ASFF appropriations allow for the purchase of ground (or diesel) and aviation fuel for the ANP. Figure 1 shows that from fiscal years 2007 through 2012, CSTC-A received approximately $499 million to purchase fuel for the ANP. For fiscal year 2013, CSTC-A requested $134.6 million for a total of more than $633 million to purchase fuel over the 7-year period. In November 2012, CSTC-A agreed to directly contribute one-third of its fiscal year 2013 ANP fuel budget to the Afghan government, which would allow MOI to purchase fuel for the ANP. By the end of 2014, when U.S. military forces complete their draw down, CSTC-A plans to contribute all of its funds for ANP fuel directly to the Afghan government.

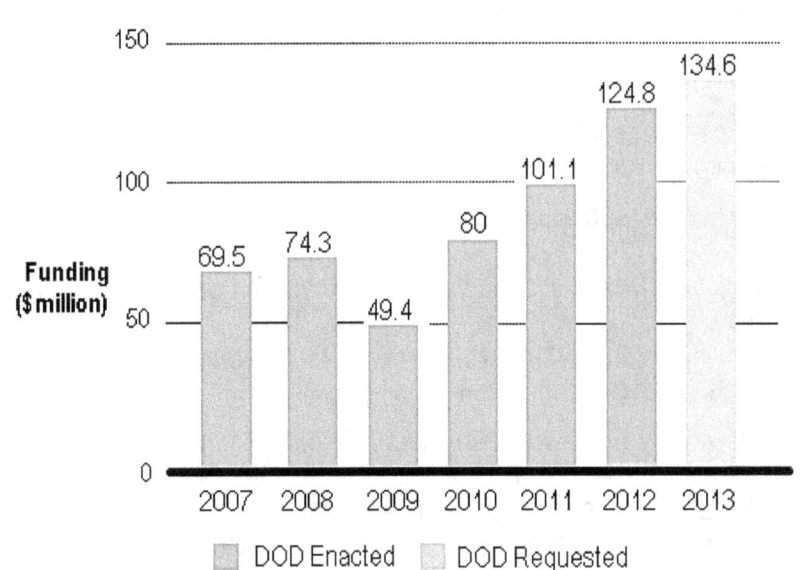

Figure 1 - Funding for ANP Fuel, Fiscal Years 2007 through 2013 (in millions)

Source: Annual Fiscal Year Justifications for Overseas Contingency Operations – Afghanistan Security Forces Fund for 2007 through 2013.

To purchase fuel for the ANP, CSTC-A uses blanket purchase agreements issued by C-JTSCC. Since 2007, C-JTSCC has established 17 blanket purchase agreements with vendors to provide fuel for the ANP and the Afghan National Army. Currently, there are agreements with eight vendors to provide ground and aviation fuel. C-JTSCC approves the monthly prices of fuel, and following that approval, CSTC-A uses the approved prices to select vendors and order fuel. These vendors then deliver directly to approximately 70 authorized ANP locations throughout Afghanistan. Once vendors deliver fuel to those 70 locations, the ANP stores and distributes the fuel to ANP district and local level units.

To account for fuel purchases and deliveries, CSTC-A created a checkbook in Microsoft Access in March 2010 to record details of fuel orders received from and directly delivered by vendors to the ANP locations. CSTC-A fuel ordering officers enter information into the checkbook, including the delivery location, fuel order number, point of contact, fuel type, fuel quantity ordered and delivered, fuel price per liter, and invoice number.

Policies and Regulations That Guide ANP Fuel Process

CSTC-A's ANP fuel program is guided by both U.S. and Afghan policies and regulations – and which policy or regulation applies depends on the stage of the fuel process. No single document provides comprehensive guidance for or establishes controls over the fuel process, leaving the purchase of ANP fuel and oversight of U.S. funds based on multiple sources.

Afghan Government Policies and Regulations

In January 2009, MOI issued its *Process for the Management of Logistics Policy*, which prescribes standards and regulations for the logistics management process,[8] and created a draft ANP fuel policy. Similar to the Ministry of Defense's logistics and petroleum, oils, and lubricants policies, MOI's logistics policy requires the following key documents to account for the request and receipt of fuel including:

- MOI Form 14—Materiel Request Form (requests fuel);
- MOI Form 8—Materiel Receiving Report (documents fuel quantity delivered);
- MOI Form 9—ANP Issue and Turn-In Order Form (issues fuel to ANP locations and serves as documentation of fuel quantity delivered).

MOI policy requires fuel requests be approved using consumption data and states that each ANP unit will account for and provide inventory and consumption data to MOI. The policy also requires units to use consumption data to forecast future fuel requirements.

U.S. Regulations and Other Guidance

In contrast, the U.S. government has contract regulations and internal control standards that guide the oversight of blanket fuel purchase agreements and fuel purchases for ANP. Fuel prices and contract costs, which are managed by C-JTSCC, are guided by U.S. regulations. The Federal Acquisition Regulation (FAR)[9] and C-JTSCC's blanket purchase agreement guidance[10] require CSTC-A, as the contracting officers representative organization, to verify and accept the quantity and quality of fuel. DOD's Material Inspection & Receiving Report (DD-250) guidance requires inspection/acceptance prior to submitting vendor invoices for payment.[11]

Standards for Internal Control in the Federal Government[12] provide the overall framework for establishing and maintaining internal control and for identifying and addressing areas of greatest risk for fraud, waste, abuse, and mismanagement. These standards note that managers should comprehensively identify risk and consider all significant interactions between the entity and other parties as well as internal factors. CSTC-A also issued standard operating procedures specifying that, prior to providing direct contributions, a risk assessment must be conducted to ensure proper stewardship of U.S. funds.

C-JTSCC AND CSTC-A EXERCISED LIMITED OVERSIGHT OF U.S. FUNDS AND FUEL PURCHASED FOR THE ANP

We found that C-JTSCC and CSTC-A had limited oversight of the contracting process for ANP fuel. C-JTSCC approved vendors' fuel prices that included costs that were unsupported or not allowed under the blanket

---

[8] MOI logistics consists of ten classes of supplies, consisting of general supplies, food, fuel, clothing, weapons, ammunition, medical and construction material, support equipment, and spare parts.

[9] FAR 13.303-5(e)(5).

[10] C-JTSCC blanket purchase agreement guidance Section II.7(2) Receipt for Deliveries.

[11] DD Form 250 Guidance for the Contractor: Source Inspection or Acceptance.

[12] United States Government Accountability Office. *Standards for Internal Control in the Federal Government*. Washington D.C.: 1999 (GAO/AIMD-00-21.3.1).

purchase agreements. Some vendors' approved prices for ground fuel included costs for the market price[13] of fuel and transportation, but the vendors did not support these costs with additional documentation. In addition, vendors charged two types of transportation fees—freight on board point and destination[14]—even though the blanket purchase agreements only allowed for destination fees. In November 2012 and December 2012, 3 of the 4 ground fuel vendors for Kabul province submitted prices that included transportation fees for ordered fuel leaving the origination point, which is prohibited under the blanket purchase agreements. The total cost of these fees totaled approximately $520,000. C-JTSCC officials stated that they were not aware vendors charged origination point fees, but also stated they considered all transportation costs allowable and the fuel prices fair and reasonable. However, C-JTSCC officials did not provide any support to justify their claims.

C-JTSCC approved vendor fuel prices that were not in compliance with the blanket purchase agreement. We found that one vendor's aviation fuel prices included costs that did not comply with the blanket purchase agreement, such as Afghan Oil Authority Fees, customs duties, government storage fees, and other costs.[15] According to the blanket purchase agreements and the U.S. Status of Forces Agreement with the Afghan government, these costs are prohibited.[16] For the period from November 2010 through February 2012, we calculated that these costs amounted to approximately $25,900.[17]

We also found that CSTC-A mostly selected vendors for ground fuel that did not provide the lowest possible price. Although CSTC-A is encouraged to select the lowest price and required to document any use of higher prices,[18] CSTC-A neither selected the vendor with the lowest fuel price each time nor documented its justification for using the higher-priced vendors. For example, from November 2012 through December 2012, CSTC-A did not choose the lowest-priced vendors for all of the 717 ground fuel orders in Kabul province. Based on our analysis, the selection of the lowest-priced vendors would have saved almost $1 million in costs over that 2-month period. According to C-JTSCC and CSTC-A officials, the higher-priced vendors were chosen because the lower-priced vendors did not obtain exemptions from taxes and duties until January 2013.[19] Still, from January 2013 through March 2013, the two lowest-priced vendors received only 435 of the 1,361 (or 32 percent) of fuel orders for ANP.

---

[13] Vendors provide the market price per metric ton of fuel each month; they are not required to support how, or from where, they derived the market price. For example, in November and December 2012, the market price per metric ton of fuel per vendor ranged from $300 to $1,150.

[14] For shipments originating outside of the U.S. for overseas delivery, the Federal Acquisition Regulation allows for freight on board point or destination fees. Freight on board point generally means that the buyer (here, the U.S.) pays costs when goods and services (i.e., fuel) leave the origination point; conversely, freight on board destination means that the U.S. does not pay until the vendor delivers the fuel. The blanket purchase agreements note clearly only freight on board destination fees should apply.

[15] In May 2013, SIGAR reported that U.S. agencies erroneously reimbursed contractors for Afghan taxes. See Special Inspector General for Afghanistan Reconstruction. *Taxes: Afghan Government Has Levied Nearly a Billion Dollars in Business Taxes on Contractors Supporting U.S. Government Efforts in Afghanistan,* Washington, D.C.: 2013 (SIGAR Audit 13-8).

[16] Blanket Purchase Agreement, Section 3.1; Agreement regarding the Status of U.S. Military and Civilian Personnel of the U.S. Department of Defense Present in Afghanistan in connection with Cooperative Efforts in Response to Terrorism, Humanitarian and Civic Assistance, Military Training and Exercises, and Other Activities, State Dept. No. 03-67, 2003 WL 21754316 (Treaty) (SOFA) ("The government of the United States of America, its military and civilian personnel, contractors and contractor personnel shall not be liable to pay any tax or similar charge assessed within Afghanistan.").

[17] SIGAR's calculation was based on CSTC-A ordering all aviation fuel worth approximately $208,226 from the vendor during this time period, which represented Afghan taxes and fees and accounted for 12.4 percent of the vendor's total approved fuel price.

[18] FAR 13.303-2(b)(2); Blanket Purchase Agreement, Statement of Work, Section 2.14.1; and C-JTSCC Blanket Purchase Agreement Guidance, Section II.6.

[19] An exemption letter is required for a contractor to be exempt from Afghanistan taxes and duties.

Without Consumption and Storage Capacity Data, CSTC-A Ordered $4.6 Million Dollars Worth of Excess Fuel for Helmand Provincial Police Headquarters

From April 2010 to March 2013, CSTC-A ordered more than 9.8 million liters of fuel, worth $17.6 million, for Helmand Provincial Police Headquarters (PHQ). The blanket purchase agreements require fuel to be delivered to only approved locations and into storage tanks designed for fuel storage. In September 2012, however, CSTC-A identified questionable and potentially fraudulent fuel deliveries to the PHQ. This involved the purported delivery of volumes of diesel fuel that exceeded Helmand PHQ's storage capacity.

MOI guidance requires that fuel consumption data be provided to justify ANP fuel needs. CSTC-A, however, does not require its staff to use consumption data from MOI when placing fuel orders.[20] In addition, CSTC-A does not have complete storage capacity information for each ANP location authorized to receive fuel directly from vendors. This resulted in instances where CSTC-A ordered and purchased the delivery of more fuel than could be stored at Helmand PHQ. For example, Regional Command Southwest officials, who have more contact with Helmand PHQ than CSTC-A fuel ordering officers because of their presence within the province, told us that Helmand PHQ had a 160,000 liter fuel storage capacity for diesel fuel. CSTC-A's checkbook recorded that vendors delivered diesel fuel in excess of 160,000 liters on 24 days over a 28-month period from June 2010 through September 2012. The deliveries on those 24 days totaled about 2.4 million liters and were worth 4.6 million. CSTC-A officials told us that Helmand PHQ's insufficient storage for all of the fuel to be delivered may have resulted in the fuel being delivered to a local market instead.

Email communications from CSTC-A officials showed that by September 2012, CSTC-A fuel ordering officers believed the unusually large monthly fuel orders "may be a case of criminal fraud." In September 2012, these fuel ordering officers referred the suspected fraud to an Army Criminal Investigation Division official, who informed them he could not investigate due to a lack of authority to bring any charges against local national or Afghan officials.

In October 2012, CSTC-A officials reduced the amount of fuel delivered to Helmand PHQ. In response, Regional Command Southwest officials, working with ANP personnel, provided CSTC-A officials with a spreadsheet that purportedly demonstrated Helmand PHQ actually had a shortage of fuel. To prove this, Regional Command Southwest officials stated they summarized MOI forms provided by ANP, which showed that Helmand PHQ distributed more fuel to district locations than it received from vendors. For example, Regional Command Southwest's spreadsheet showed that from March 20, 2012 to April 20, 2012,[21] Helmand PHQ distributed 439,836 liters after receiving only 415,000 liters from vendors, resulting in a shortage of 24,386 liters.

However, our analysis of CSTC-A's checkbook showed that Regional Command Southwest officials' claims of Helmand PHQ's fuel shortage lacked credibility because CSTC-A reported more fuel being delivered to Helmand PHQ than claimed by the Regional Command Southwest officials. We found that Helmand PHQ received 535,000 liters of fuel from vendors, approximately 120,000 liters more than Regional Command Southwest officials reported to CSTC-A officials. In addition, CSTC-A officials were not present at most delivery points and did not receive MOI forms that would allow them to verify when, how and if Helmand PHQ distributed fuel to the locations it claimed. CSTC-A officials should have identified the significant difference between the volume of fuel reported by Regional Command Southwest officials for that period and the volume reported delivered by fuel vendors. As noted in figure 2, by December 2012, CSTC-A increased the monthly fuel deliveries to Helmand PHQ to 300,000 liters without addressing the fuel requirement needed or investigating the fraud allegations.

---

[20] All fuel requests are approved by MOI and submitted to CSTC-A.

[21]The 30-day Afghan month is based on the Afghan year, which starts on March, 20th.

Figure 2 - ANP Helmand PHQ Monthly Fuel Orders, April 2010 through March 2013 (in thousands of liters)

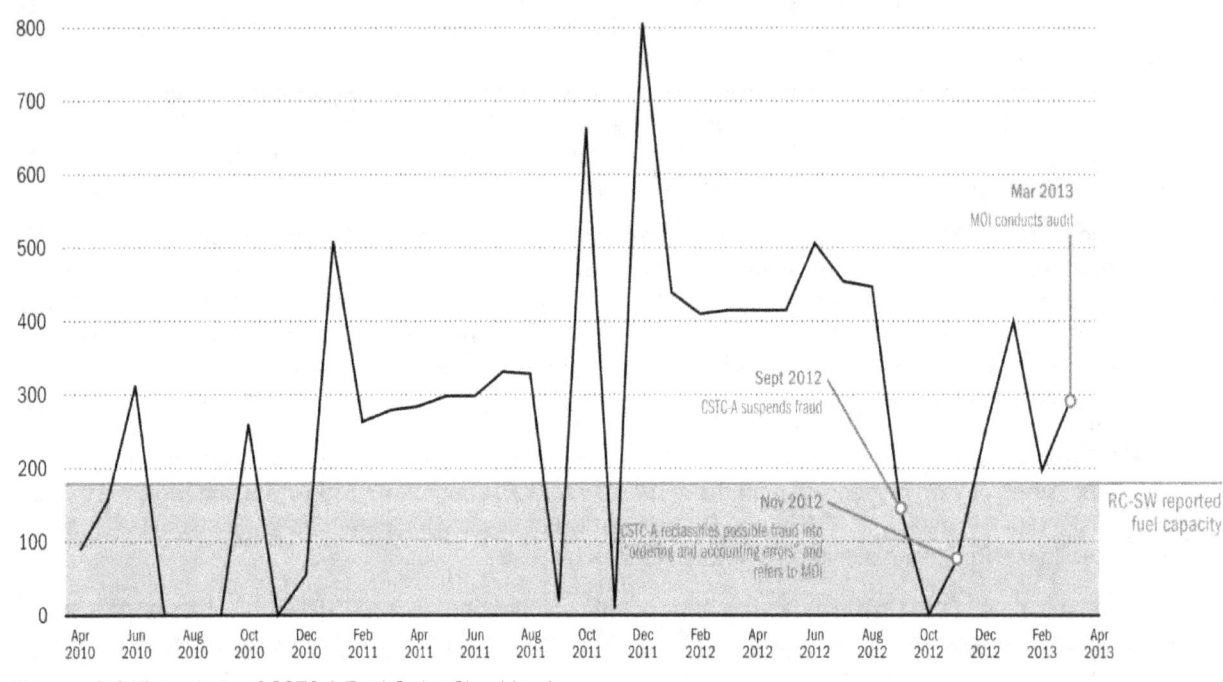

Source: SIGAR analysis of CSTC-A Fuel Order Checkbook

CSTC-A not only resumed placing large orders for Helmand PHQ by December 2012, but redefined its suspicion of fraud as "ordering and accounting errors." In November 2012, a CSTC-A brigadier general sent a letter to a MOI brigadier general that characterized the Helmand PHQ case as an "isolated incident" and requested MOI to conduct an audit of Helmand PHQ's fuel management procedures.[22] As of May 2013, the results of the MOI audit were not available, but the Combined Joint Interagency Task Force-Shafafiyat, whose representatives accompanied MOI on the audit, identified weaknesses in Helmand PHQ's fuel management and concluded that a follow up visit would be needed. As of May 2013, no other audit or investigation had been conducted into whether any U.S.-purchased fuel was lost to waste, fraud, or abuse – including the possible diversion of excess fuel to a local market.[23]

CSTC-A DID NOT PERFORM RISK ASSESSMENTS OR VERIFY THE AFGHAN GOVERNMENT'S USE OF $26.8 MILLION OF DIRECT BUDGETARY CONTRIBUTIONS OF U.S. FUNDS

Since October 2011, CSTC-A has directly contributed $26.8 million of U.S. funds to the Afghan government and plans to directly contribute another $1.2 billion over the next 5 years for the purchase of fuel for ANP. CSTC-A's standard operating procedures require six steps be taken prior to the disbursement of direct contributions, including a risk assessment and steps to verify how direct contributions are spent. However, we could not find evidence that CSTC-A officials conducted the required risk assessment to determine MOI's readiness to assume all responsibilities for capacity development and stewardship of U.S. funds. Although CSTC-A had one power point slide that referred to a risk assessment and indicated that direct contributions for ANP fuel were rated as "high-risk," CSTC-A officials approved $243 million for direct contributions to the Afghan government for fiscal year 2014. CSTC-A officials stated they did not have a plan to mitigate the risk and could not provide further documentation or explanation for the rating. Additionally, in April 2012, DOD reported that the "ANP

---

[22] Two other CSTC-A generals issued similar letters between November 2012 and January 2013.

[23] On May 7, 2013, we referred this matter to SIGAR's Investigations Directorate for further examination.

logistics system requires significant coalition assistance at the regional level and below in order to effectively sustain the ANP." Similarly, in December 2012, DOD reported that although the ANP logistics system has made steady progress toward self-sufficiency, major challenges remain. According to its July 2013 report, DOD does not expect MOI to be ready to assume complete responsibility for all logistics functions until the third quarter of 2014.[24]

Although CSTC-A did not have a plan to mitigate the risk of waste, fraud, and abuse of its direct funding to the Afghan government, it continued to provide direct funding. As shown in figure 3, between October 2011 and August 2012, CSTC-A transferred the initial $10.6 million to the Afghan government for MOI to purchase fuel for ANP. In February and September 2012, the Army Audit Agency reported that limited controls were in place to ensure visibility and accountability over ASFF direct contributions and that a lack of documentation prevented the audit of the initial direct funding. In December 2012, CSTC-A transferred another $16.2 million to purchase fuel for ANP, to cover the period from December 21, 2012 through December 20, 2013. In October 2012, CSTC-A revised its direct contribution standard operating procedures to improve controls by addressing issues raised by the U.S. Army Audit Agency. The procedures require CSTC-A staff to perform periodic reconciliations, audits, and reporting of how MOI spends U.S. funds.[25] In May 2013, CSTC-A officials stated they will not implement the revised procedures to determine how MOI uses the $16.2 million until MOI awards contracts to initiate its own purchase of fuel for ANP.[26] As a result, CSTC-A cannot yet determine how the Afghan government used the additional $16.2 million to purchase fuel, and we could not evaluate the effectiveness of CSTC-A's new control procedures.

Figure 3 - ANP Direct Contribution History

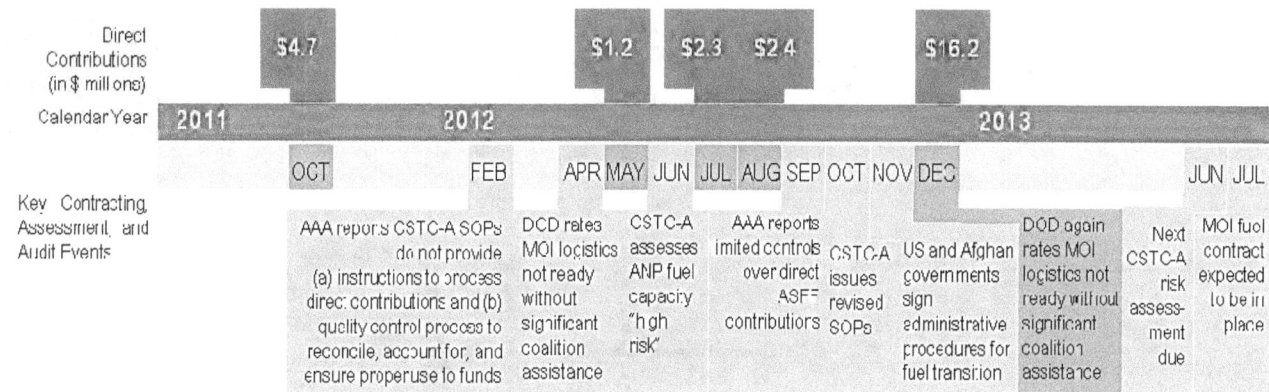

Source: SIGAR analysis of key contracting, assessment, and audit events.
Notes: AAA–U.S. Army Audit Agency; SOP–Standard Operating Procedures.

---

[24] DOD Report on Progress Toward Security and Stability in Afghanistan, dated April 2012, December 2012, and July 2013.

[25] In November 2012, the International Security Assistance Force, CSTC-A, and Afghanistan Ministries of Interior, Finance, and Commerce and Industry signed the Administrative Procedures for Bulk Fuel Management Transition (Procedures). The Procedures transition financing, contracting, and ordering ANP fuel from the Coalition to the Afghan government and require CSTC-A to audit the ANP fuel process and MOI to audit the ANP fuel distribution, consumption, supply, and accountability. The Procedures also require MOI to provide storage capacity for fuel and documentation to support vendor payments to CSTC-A.

[26] During the time of our fieldwork, MOI had not awarded contracts to purchase fuel for ANP.

CSTC-A OVERSTATED FUNDING ESTIMATES FOR ANP FUEL BY ABOUT $94 MILLION FOR FISCAL YEAR 2013

The basis for CSTC-A's fiscal year 2013 ANP fuel funding request and future funding estimates is questionable. As shown in figure 4, in fiscal year 2013, CSTC-A requested $134.6 million to purchase fuel for ANP, one-third (about $45 million) of which will be a direct contribution to the Afghan government.[27] CSTC-A also plans to provide all of the fiscal years 2014 through 2018 fuel funding requirements—currently estimated by CSTC-A at more than $1.2 billion over those 5 years—directly to the Afghan government. Although MOI guidance requires ANP units to track their fuel consumption to determine future fuel requirements, CSTC-A did not receive or use ANP unit consumption data in developing funding requirements for ANP fuel. Instead, CSTC-A used previously reported ANP fuel orders and assumptions to estimate future requirements for ANP fuel. However, CSTC-A did not provide support for those assumptions as required by federal internal control standards.[28]

Figure 4 - Budget Request and Estimates for ANP Fuel, Fiscal Years 2013 through 2018 (in millions)

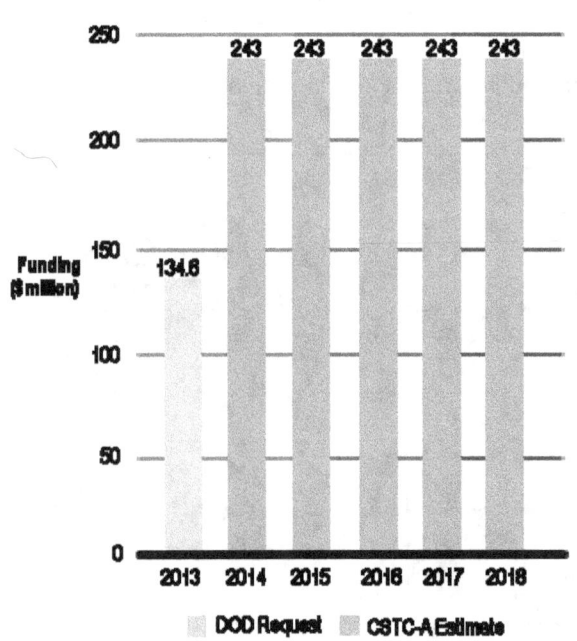

Source: Fiscal Year Justification for Overseas Contingency Operations – Afghanistan Security Forces Fund for 2013 and fiscal years 2014-2018 Program Objective Memorandum Afghanistan Security Forces Fund Appropriation Requirements and Resourcing Development Sheet.

For example, CSTC-A officials did not have reliable information on the number of vehicles and generators or their use, at ANP locations. CSTC-A officials assumed ANP's fuel requirements would remain steady after the U.S. military role ceases by the end of 2014. To explain their methodology, CSTC-A officials directed us to a June 2011 briefing slide and September 2012 memo that notes costs for fuel are based on last year's "consumption," multiplied by a "fielding inflation factor" and an "operational tempo factor." According to CSTC-

---

[27] On November 13, 2012, the U.S. and Afghan governments signed Administrative Procedures for the Bulk Fuel Management Transition, which established a one-third direct contribution maximum of $62.6 million for fiscal year 2013. The maximum contribution is based on an estimated total annual ANP fuel requirement of $189.6 million, which includes an unsupported projected annual "ANP Operational Tempo" increase of 16 percent.

[28] United States Government Accountability Office. *Standards for Internal Control in the Federal Government*: 1999 (GAO/AIMD-00-21.3.1). The Control Activities section on Appropriate Documentation of Transactions and Internal Control states that internal control and all transactions need to be clearly documented.

A officials, no other information existed on the fielding and operational tempo factor notations. Further, CSTC-A officials could not provide additional information or documentation that would better support the $134.6 million request or the future estimates. Although the slide used the term "consumption," CSTC-A officials confirmed this actually meant past fuel orders. As a result, CSTC-A has estimated a combined $1.4 billion of funding requirements for the six years, which are based on the ANP's past orders, including those questioned at Helmand PHQ. Relying on past orders fails to take into account whether some fuel was lost, stolen, or not used as intended.

Based on our analysis, CSTC-A overstated its fiscal year 2013 funding request for ANP fuel by approximately $94 million, as it had a significant amount of the previous year's funds available well into fiscal year 2013.[29] CSTC-A requested $134.6 million for fiscal year 2013, and based on ANP's fiscal year 2012 orders, we determined that the average value of fuel orders per month was $13.5 million. By the end of fiscal year 2012, however, CSTC-A had its entire fiscal year 2012 budget—$124.8 million—still available. At a rate of $13.5 million per month, $124.8 million will cover 9 months' worth of fuel in fiscal year 2013—from October 2012 through June 2013. The remaining 3 months of fiscal year 2013, July 2013 through September 2013, will require approximately $40 million. In other words, CSTC-A needs $40 million of its $134 million request to cover the 3-month period, leaving $94 million that would be available for other uses.

CONCLUSION

The ANP fuel program managed by C-JTSCC and CSTC-A remains at high risk of loss, theft, or misuse of U.S. funds and purchased fuel and, if not improved, may increasingly place large amounts of U.S. funds at risk of fraud, waste, and abuse. Until C-JTSCC and CSTC-A improve controls, verify fuel prices, and determine that fuel orders are in line with consumption and storage capacities at ANP sites, neither entity can assure that U.S. funds and fuel are used as intended. Moreover, without consumption and storage capacity information from MOI, CSTC-A has no basis for assuming that ANP fuel orders are legitimate. Until CSTC-A performs a risk assessment and implements effective audit and other oversight procedures, to mitigate the risk associated with direct budgetary contributions of U.S. funds to the Afghan government to purchase fuel for ANP, it will continue to provide significant funds without any assurance that MOI can provide proper stewardship of U.S. funds. Lastly, without a sound methodology to determine budget estimates that includes consumption data, CSTC-A will not be able to accurately identify ANP fuel requirements. Continuing this approach will likely result in significant amounts of the unused funds being available well into subsequent fiscal years and CSTC-A may continue to provide Congress with inaccurate budget requests and estimates for ANP fuel.

RECOMMENDATIONS

To ensure the reasonableness of prices for ANP fuel, we recommend that the Commander of C-JTSCC:

1. Review and determine whether all vendor fuel prices since 2007, and related transportation costs and Afghan taxes, fees and duties, were allowable and seek recovery of any disallowed costs.

2. Develop guidance that details the factors to be considered when not selecting the lowest-priced fuel vendors, and enforce C-JTSCC's guidance requiring justification, in writing, for the selection of higher-priced vendors when lower-cost vendors are available.

To improve oversight of U.S. funding for ANP fuel, we recommend that the Commander of CSTC-A:

3. Obtain fuel consumption and storage capacity data for each of the 70 authorized ANP locations receiving fuel directly from vendors.

---

[29] The Afghanistan Security Forces Fund is a two-year appropriation. For instance, the fiscal year 2012 funds remain available from October 2011 through September 2013.

4. Ensure that consumption data is used by MOI to approve all fuel orders.

5. Review fuel ordering levels, consumption data, and storage capacity for each of the 70 ANP locations and determine whether other ANP locations are receiving fuel above their storage capacity. If fuel orders are above storage capacity, subsequent fuel orders for that location should be adjusted to not exceed storage capacity and excess fuel deliveries should be investigated.

To improve compliance with CSTC-A direct contribution standard operating procedures, we recommend that the Commander of CSTC-A:

6. Perform the required risk assessments and monitor the effectiveness of the new reconciliation, auditing, and reporting requirements and document these actions.

To improve ANP fuel budget estimates for the current and future fiscal years, we recommend that the Commander of CSTC-A:

7. Reduce the fiscal year 2013 request to that required for 3 months–$ 40.6 million—to correspond with the 12-month fiscal year fuel requirement for ANP, which ends September 30, 2013 and put the remaining $94 million to better use within Afghanistan Security Forces Fund.

8. Obtain and use fuel consumption data from all ANP units as a basis to revise fuel budget estimates for fiscal years 2014 through 2018.

AGENCY COMMENTS

SIGAR received formal comments on a draft of this report from C-JTSCC and CSTC-A. C-JTSCC concurred with the two recommendations addressed to it and CSTC-A concurred with five of the six recommendations addressed to it. Both C-JTSCC and CSTC-A provided additional technical comments, which we incorporated into the report, as appropriate.

Although C-JTSCC concurred with the recommendation to review and determine whether vendor fuel prices were allowable, it also stated that all fuel prices and related transportation costs and Afghan taxes, fees and duties were allowable under the blanket purchase agreements since 2007. According to C-JTSCC, the contractors' submitted prices were fixed, and no costs other than the fixed rates were allowable or ever paid in any of the blanket purchase agreements. However, we found that the monthly fixed prices, approved by C-JTSCC, included costs that were unallowable under the blanket purchase agreement, including transportation costs for freight on board point, Afghan Oil Authority fees, customs duties, government storage fees, 2-percent business receipt tax, and municipality and toll charges. Because only freight on board destination costs were allowable and the fuel deliveries were exempt from Afghan taxes and fees per blanket purchase agreements and the U.S.–Afghan Status of Forces Agreement, we maintain that these costs should not be charged to the government as part of the fixed prices, and should be recovered.

In its comments, CSTC-A noted several actions it is taking to address our recommendations. For example, CSTC-A concurred with SIGAR's recommendation to ensure that consumption data is used by MOI to approve all fuel orders, and CSTC-A stated that it has published an approved schedule to conduct periodic audits of the entire fuel order approval process to ensure MOI continues to use appropriate consumption documentation to validate fuel orders. Regarding SIGAR's recommendation to perform the required risk assessments, CSTC-A stated it would treat POL as a "high-risk program," plan audits, and require the ANP to track these transition POL contracts to allow better oversight and accountability of funds. However, we maintain that a risk assessment is needed to ensure that ANP has the capacity and capability to manage U.S. funds and fuel purchases. With regard to SIGAR's recommendation to reduce the fiscal year 2013 request, CSTC-A agreed to lower the requirement to $40.6 million and put the remaining $94 million to better use within ASFF. CSTC-A added that before releasing direct contributions funds it will apply due diligence to the estimated amounts required.

Finally, CSTC-A concurred with our recommendation to obtain and use fuel consumption data from all ANP units as a basis for revising fuel budget estimates for fiscal years 2014 through 2018. Moreover, CSTC-A stated that if an ANP unit is suspected of diverting fuel to unapproved storage locations, it would suspend fuel ordering until the discrepancy is resolved.

CSTC-A did not agree with our recommendation to review fuel ordering levels, consumption data, and storage capacity data to ensure that fuel is not delivered in excess of an ANP sites' fuel storage capacity. CSTC-A stated that because this information is not real-time data, it does not facilitate ordering decisions. Moreover, CSTC-A stated it is unrealistic in the current operating environment to monitor fuel tank status for each of the units receiving direct delivery of fuel. We concur with CSTC-A on this point, and did not recommend that CSTC-A do so. CSTC-A's explanation for its nonoccurrence with Recommendation 5 does not address the concerns raised by SIGAR. In particular, CSTC-A stated that "ANP units have been advised to increase the frequency of ordering to replace fuel consumed over an established period of days, in order to mitigate the risk of placing large, established quantity orders on a set timetable." The problem with this approach is that it can still lead to a unit placing orders that exceed storage capacity, as evidenced in this report's discussion of the Helmand PHQ. Therefore, we maintain that it is vital for CSTC-A to review the consumption data and storage capacity data to establish fuel ordering levels and determine if fuel deliveries are in excess of the fuel storage capacity of each ANP unit.

APPENDIX I - SCOPE AND METHODOLOGY

In September 2012, the Office of the Special Inspector General for Afghanistan Reconstruction (SIGAR) identified two issues during its audit of the Afghan National Army's logistics capability for fuel. The two issues warranted immediate attention related to the short timeframes for the transfer of Afghan National Army fuel responsibilities and the direct transfer of U.S. funds to the Afghan government and challenges with upcoming budget decisions (see SIGAR Interim ANA fuel Report 12-14 issued September 10, 2012 and final Afghan National Army fuel Audit Report 13-4 issued January 2013). We initiated this audit to evaluate U.S. oversight of fuel purchases for the Afghan National Police (ANP). This report assesses (1) the extent to which U.S. Central Command Joint Theatre Support Contracting Command (C-JTSCC) and the Combined Security Transition Command-Afghanistan (CSTC-A) provided oversight of ANP fuel purchases, deliveries, and consumption, (2) CSTC-A's efforts to provide direct contributions to the Afghan government to support ANP's logistics transition, and (3) the basis and support of CSTC-A's funding request for fiscal year 2013 and its estimates from fiscal years 2014 through 2018 for ANP fuel.

To assess C-JTSCC's and CSTC-A's oversight of ANP fuel purchases, deliveries, and consumption, we reviewed the Ministry of Interior (MOI) Logistics Policy, related Department of Defense (DOD) guidance, the Federal Acquisition Regulation, and the required MOI and DOD forms and other documentation. We also considered the fuel blanket purchase agreements awarded in November 2012 to evaluate CSTC-A revised policies and procedures developed to address performance and accountability issues identified during our Afghan National Army fuel audit. We also reviewed the U.S. Army Audit Agency audit of CSTC-A's direct contributions and interviewed CSTC-A, C-JSTCC, Defense Finance and Accounting Services, MOI, and U.S. Army Audit Agency officials to obtain an understanding of controls in place for the ANP fuel process.

To assess CSTC-A's efforts to provide direct contributions to the Afghan government to support ANP's logistics transition, we reviewed CSTC-A's direct contribution standard operating procedures, fragmentary orders, risk assessments, and direct contribution letters, DOD's MOI capability milestone ratings, and the U.S. and Afghan bulk fuel management transition administrative procedures. We reviewed and analyzed MOI logistics policies and procedures, blanket purchase agreements, and CSTC-A, U.S. Army Audit Agency, and Task Force 2010 fuel presentation slides. We also analyzed CSTC-A reported issues and DOD Inspector General audit reports and interviewed officials at CSTC-A, MOI's Material Management Center, Task Force 2010, and Defense Logistics Agency to obtain the status of identified challenges and issues to develop a capable and sustainable ANP fuel processes, and to determine the level of risk associated with ANP fuel.

To assess the basis and support of CSTC-A's funding request for fiscal year 2013 and its estimates from fiscal years 2014 through 2018 for ANP fuel, we examined DOD's Afghanistan Security Forces Fund fiscal year 2012 and 2013 budget justifications, CSTC-A's Afghanistan Security Forces Fund Requirements and Resourcing Development Sheets for fiscal years 2013-2017 and 2014-2018, and the available supporting documentation used to estimate annual funding levels. We interviewed CSTC-A officials and analyzed CSTC-A's ANP fuel ordering checkbook and CSTC-A, C-JTSCC, and Defense Finance and Accounting Service's available fuel financial data.

In an attempt to assess the reliability of the ANP fuel and financial related data, we reviewed and attempted to reconcile (1) CSTC-A's fuel ordering office checkbook of invoiced ANP fuel orders, (2) C-JTSCC's purchase requisition and commitment reported ANSF fuel order calls for payment, (3) CSTC-A's ANSF fuel vendor obligations and payments, and (4) Defense Finance and Accounting Services' computer-generated payment data. Due to no ANSF fuel data for fiscal years 2005, ANSF fuel data only for fiscal years 2006-2009, and differences in ANP fuel data for fiscal years 2011 to current, we determined the available data was either not adequately supported or not reliable for the intended purposes of our audit. However, we assessed internal controls over the ANP fuel processes and considered allegations of fraud through review of CSTC-A briefings and documentation of fuel contracts, orders, and payments. The results of our reconciliation and assessments are included in the body of this report.

We conducted our audit work in Kabul, Afghanistan from September 2012 to September 2013, in accordance with generally accepted government auditing standards. Those standards require that we plan and perform the audit to obtain sufficient, appropriate evidence to provide a reasonable basis for our findings and conclusions based on our audit objectives. We believe that the evidence obtained provides a reasonable basis for our findings and conclusions based on our audit objectives. SIGAR conducted this audit under the authority of Public Law No. 110-181, as amended, and the Inspector General Act of 1978, as amended.

APPENDIX II - AGENCY COMMENTS FROM U.S. CENTRAL COMMAND JOINT THEATER SUPPORT CONTRACTING COMMAND

HEADQUARTERS
CENTCOM JOINT THEATER SUPPORT CONTRACTING COMMAND
CAMP PHOENIX
APO AE 09320

CJTSCC/DCO   17 September 2013

MEMORANDUM FOR CCIG

SUBJECT: SIGAR Draft Report 13-20 - "ANP Fuel program - concerted effort needed to strengthen oversight"

1. It was recommended that C-JTSCC review and determine whether all vendor fuel prices since 2007, and related transportation costs and Afghan taxes, fees and duties, were allowable and seek recovery of any disallowed costs. Response: Concur. C-JTSCC reviewed and determined that all vendor fuel prices under the previous blanket purchase agreements (BPAs) and related transportation costs and Afghan taxes, fees and duties, were allowable.

   a. The contracting vehicle used to procure fuel in support of the Afghan National Army and Afghan National Police until 31 August 2013 was a blanket purchase agreement (BPA). Within the BPAs, contractors submitted price lists at a fixed price per liter of fuel for each of the Afghan Districts. The fixed price did not segregate various costs that the contractor may incur. Instead it was a fixed rate for the delivery of fuel to a particular district. No costs other than the fixed rates were allowable or ever paid in any of the blanket purchase agreements.

   b. Paragraph 1.1.1 in the Statement of Work states the fixed price includes delivery to the destination. None of the fuel BPA contractors ever invoiced for or were paid transportation costs other than those included in their fixed price. The memorandum for record from GSCC dated 21 May 2013, titled "SIGAR Statement of Facts Oversight of Afghan National Police Fuel Management (070A)" fully addresses in paragraph 3 that the government paid only for the fuel delivered at the agreed upon rate per liter. The government never paid additional delivery costs for the fuel.

   c. All fuel deliveries were exempt from Afghanistan taxes, levies, and duties since the commodity was purchased by the US Government for use by GIRoA, in accordance with FAR 52.229-6, DFARS 252.229-7000, and local clause 952.225-0019. As such, contractors were instructed to not include any taxes, levies, or duties in the calculation of their pricing. Also, paragraph 3.1 in the Statement of Work explicitly prohibited contractors from including any Afghan taxes, levies, or cuties in the price of their fuel. The fuel BPA contractors never invoiced for or were reimbursed for taxes, levies, or duties. The government only paid for the fuel that was delivered at the agreed upon rate per liter.

2. It was recommended that C-JTSCC develop guidance that details the factors to be considered when not selecting the lowest-priced vendors to promote adherence to C-JTSCC's guidance requiring justification, in writing, on the selection of higher-priced vendors when lower-cost vendors are available. Response: Concur. C-JTSCC addressed the factors considered when not selecting the lowest-priced and identified that the contractor has the "right to refuse" accepting BPA calls. C-JTSCC also offered scenarios when the contractor might choose to do so.

   a. BPA calls were always offered first to the lowest priced BPA holder. However, in a blanket purchase agreement, the contractor has the right to refuse accepting a BPA call. Typically they would do so because of a low inventory of fuel, they were already executing multiple calls and did not have the operational capability, or they experienced other internal factors that prevented them from accepting the BPA calls. When this occurred, the ordering officer would place the order with the next lowest priced contractor.

b. As of 1 September 2013, C-JTSCC procures fuel in support of the ANSF with IDIQ (indefinite delivery, indefinite quantity) contracts. In an IDIQ contract, the contractor does not have the right to refuse delivery orders. Also, the IDIQs are centralized, which means the contracting officer will determine which contractor has the lowest price, instead of the ordering officer. Each delivery order is competitively awarded based upon price.

3. Questions regarding this memo can be addressed to C-JTSCC/Contract Support, Plans, and Operations (C-SPO) at ███████████████████████████

CAPT Linda
Schlesinger

Linda Schlesinger
CAPT, USN
Deputy Commander

HEADQUARTERS
COMBINED SECURITY TRANSITION COMMAND - AFGHANISTAN
MINISTERIAL ADVISORY GROUP
KABUL, AFGHANISTAN
APO AE 09356

REPLY TO
ATTENTION OF
CSTC-A   11 SEP 2013

MEMORANDUM THRU   United States Forces - Afghanistan (CJIG), APO AE 09356
                                 United States Central Command (CCIG), MacDill AFB, FL 33621

FOR: Special Inspector General for Afghanistan Reconstruction, 2530 Crystal Drive, Arlington, VA 22202-3940

SUBJECT: CSTC-A MAG Draft Response to SIGAR Draft Report: "Afghan National Police Fuel Program: Concerted Efforts Needed to Strengthen Oversight of U.S. Funds" (SIGAR Draft Report 13-20).

REFERENCE: Draft Report, dated SEP 2013, Special Inspector General for Afghanistan Reconstruction (SIGAR).

1. The purpose of this memorandum is to provide draft responses on the SIGAR Draft Report.

2. Point of contact for this action is CPT Matthew E. French at DSN ████████, or via e-mail at ██████████████████████

KEVIN R. WENDEL
Major General, US Army
Commanding General

Enclosure:
CSTC-A MAG Draft Report Response

CSTC-A MAG DRAFT REPORT RESPONSE
"Afghan National Police Fuel Program: Concerted Efforts Needed to Strengthen Oversight of
U.S. Funds"
(SIGAR Draft Report 13-20)

1. Recommendation 3:
The Commander, Combined Security Transition Command-Afghanistan, obtain fuel
consumption and storage capacity data for each of the 145 authorized ANP locations receiving
fuel directly from vendors.

CSTC-A response:

a. CSTC-A concurs with the SIGAR recommendation to obtain fuel consumption and
storage capacity data for each of the 145 (now 70) authorized ANP locations receiving
fuel directly from vendors.

> See SIGAR
> Comment 1

b. Upon CSTC-A's recommendation, MoI published a cipher directing an additional
reduction of sites receiving direct delivery of fuel from 145 sites to 70. This action
allows greater oversight of ANP fuel deliveries by the remaining coalition advisors.

c. Per MoI Fuel Policy (2.1.2), MoI Form 32s documenting monthly consumption are
required to be provided to MMC-P along with each MoI Form 14 requesting fuel.
However, unlike DLA-E standard operating procedures, MoI does not have an
automated method for obtaining accurate consumption data at each retail fuel point.
All consumption data is obtained from frontline ANP policemen and recorded
manually on MoI Form 3643. The consumption documentation process is often
ignored by the ANP which skews the estimate data. Because CSTC-A does not have
direct authority over ANP units or the ability to enforce individual adherence to
policy, CSTC-A is left to rely upon inaccurate estimate data provided by ANP units.

d. CSTC-A has received estimates of each direct delivery site's storage capacity from
coalition advisors. Storage capacity data is described as an "estimate" because many
sites utilize non-standard tanks that do not have accompanying strapping charts (depict
storage capacity data), as well as static fuel tankers that function as bulk storage. As a
site's number of individual tanks functioning as bulk storage increase, the amount of
functional storage lost to unobtainables and ullage increases as well. Therefore, relying
just on site storage capacities based upon both standard and non-standard gross rated
tank capacities is not entirely reliable.

Page 1 of 5

CSTC-A MAG DRAFT REPORT RESPONSE
"Afghan National Police Fuel Program: Concerted Efforts Needed to Strengthen Oversight of
U.S. Funds"
(SIGAR Draft Report 13-20)

2. Recommendation 4:
The Commander, Combined Security Transition Command-Afghanistan, ensure that
consumption data is used by MoI to approve all fuel orders.

CSTC-A response:

    a. CSTC-A concurs with the SIGAR recommendation to ensure that consumption data is
    used by MoI to approve all fuel orders.

    b. Per IJC Daily FRAGO 17-08-13, CSTC-A published an approved schedule to conduct
    periodic audits of the entire fuel order approval process, to be conducted at the middle
    and end of fiscal years in conjunction with both the MoI Inspector General and
    Shafafiyat. CSTC-A will ensure MoI continues to utilize appropriate consumption
    documentation to validate fuel orders.

3. Recommendation 5:
The Commander, Combined Security Transition Command-Afghanistan, review fuel ordering
levels, consumption data, and storage capacity for each of the 145 ANP locations and determine
whether other ANP locations are receiving fuel above their storage capacity. If fuel orders are
above storage capacity, subsequent fuel orders for that location should be adjusted to not exceed
storage capacity and excess fuel deliveries should be investigated.

CSTC-A response:

    a. CSTC-A does not concur with the SIGAR recommendation to review fuel ordering
    levels, consumption data and storage capacity for each of the 145 ANP locations and
    determine whether other ANP locations are receiving fuel above their storage capacity.

    b. Per DCOM-SPO FRAGO 12-141, coalition advisors are required to upload ANSF fuel
    consumption data on a monthly basis. However, because this information is not real-
    time data, it does not facilitate ordering decisions, especially for upcoming
    requirements. It is unrealistic, in the current operating environment, to require CSTC-
    A to monitor tank status for each of the 70 ANP units receiving direct delivery of fuel
    due to the dearth of reliable, up-to-date inventory data. Moreover, because of the delay
    in MoI Form 14 approval, any information provided by units at the time of submission
    is no longer accurate. It is incumbent upon the ANP internal supply chain managers to
    maintain positive inventory control on MoI Form 1235 (Bulk Fuel Physical Inventory
    Document).

    c. Per MoI Fuel Policy (2.1.1), each site is provided with a validated fuel allocation by
    MMC-P. This is a monthly maximum amount of fuel that is allowed to be ordered by
    each unit. This allocation is calculated by multiplying each vehicle and generator on

Page 2 of 5

the individual unit's *tashkil* by a standard fuel consumption factor for each item. Any
site that attempts to exceed this allocation will be denied fuel until the next month. A
site may justify exceeding this amount only by exception and with strong justification
showing an increase in mission or other extenuating circumstances. Any increase
must be approved by the MoI Director of Logistics.

d. CSTC-A, via Log Sync VTC, advocated the establishment of individual Inventory
Management Plans for each unit. This guidance will be incorporated into the MoI Fuel
Policy currently under review. ANP units have been advised to establish an
emergency fuel reserve level as well as emergency reorder points. ANP units have also
been advised to increase the frequency of ordering to replace fuel consumed over an
established period of days unique to each unit's need. This ordering method will
mitigate the risk of placing large, established quantity orders on a set timetable, which
can lead to a unit placing orders which exceed storage capacity.

e. If an ANP unit is suspected of diverting fuel to unapproved storage locations, CSTC-A
will suspend fuel ordering for that unit until the discrepancy can be resolved. At this
point, CSTC-A is required to verify that the fuel order in question fulfills an
operational need and is not based upon allocation alone.

4. Recommendation 6:
The Commander, Combined Security Transition Command-Afghanistan, perform the required
risk assessments and monitor the effectiveness of the new reconciliation, auditing, and reporting
requirements and document these actions.

CSTC-A response:

a. CSTC-A concurs with the SIGAR recommendation to perform the required risk
assessments and monitor the effectiveness of the new reconciliation, auditing, and
reporting requirements and document these actions.

b. Currently, CJIATF-Shafafiyat conducts audits on POL provided via US contracts to
the ANP. The ANP have not yet awarded the fuel contract planned for FY13. As
such, CSTC-A has not funded ANP fuel via direct contributions. Upon POL contract
transition to direct contributions, most likely during FY14, CSTC-A CJ8 will treat
POL as a 'high-risk program' and will conduct the requisite periodic audits. The
current plan is to require the ANP to track these transition POL contracts in AFMIS to
allow better oversight and accountability of funds.

Page 3 of 5

5. Recommendation 7:
The Commander, Combined Security Transition Command-Afghanistan, reduce the fiscal year
2013 request to that required for 3 months--$ 40.6 million—to correspond with the 12-month
fiscal year fuel requirement for ANP, which ends September 30, 2013 and put the remaining $94
million to better use within Afghanistan Security Forces Fund.

CSTC-A response:

a. CSTC-A concurs with the SIGAR recommendation to reduce the fiscal year 2013
request to that required for 3 months--$ 40.6 million—to correspond with the 12-
month fiscal year fuel requirement for ANP, which ends September 30, 2013 and put
the remaining $94 million to better use within Afghanistan Security Forces Fund.

b. ASFF is a 2-year appropriation and no FY13 funds have been provided to-date as
direct contributions to MoI. Currently, best estimates put POL transition in the
January 2014 timeframe. Before releasing direct contribution funds in support of
Afghan contracts for POL, CSTC-A will certainly apply due diligence to the estimated
amounts required.

6. Recommendation 8:
The Commander, Combined Security Transition Command-Afghanistan, obtains and uses fuel
consumption data from all ANP units as a basis to revise fuel budget estimates for fiscal years
2014 through 2018.

CSTC-A response:

a. CSTC-A concurs with the SIGAR recommendation to obtain and use fuel
consumption data from all ANP units as a basis to revise fuel budget estimates for
fiscal years 2014 through 2018.

b. Per IJC Daily FRAGO 17-08-13, a periodic audit schedule will help establish the
veracity of the fuel ordering documentation.

c. Per MoI Fuel Policy, MMC-P validates all fuel orders based upon consumption data
provided by MoI Form 32. Therefore, all orders validated and approved by MMC-P
can be viewed as supported by consumption documents. As CSTC-A does not place
any orders that have not been validated by MMC-P; historical ordering information
can be seen as a reasonably reliable predictor of future requirements.

d. For the requirements for outyears 14-18, CSTC-A used a generator study and a ANP
ground fuel summary to determine bulk fuel requirements. The RRD is the document
for ANP and was used as basis for POM requirements.

Page 4 of 5

e. CSTC-A identified unjustifiable cost growth in fuel requirements when preparing the FY15 requirement. CSTC-A reduced the requirement by $57M based on further analysis.

f. CSTC-A is revalidating the fuel requirements for FY15 during program review this fall. This review will identify fuel reduction opportunities to help the Afghans become self-sufficient.

APPROVED BY:
SEAN L. CASSIDY
COL, DCOM-SPO
DEPUTY COMMANDER

PREPARED BY:
ANDREW V. GILL
Capt, USAF
Class III Staff Officer, DSN ████████

Page 5 of 5

1. SIGAR revised the recommendation to reflect the new, lower number of authorized ANP locations.

APPENDIX IV - ACKNOWLEDGMENTS

Preston S. Heard, Senior Program Manager

Steven R. Haughton, Auditor-in-Charge

Christina M. Andersson, Senior Analyst

| SIGAR's Mission | The mission of the Special Inspector General for Afghanistan Reconstruction (SIGAR) is to enhance oversight of programs for the reconstruction of Afghanistan by conducting independent and objective audits, inspections, and investigations on the use of taxpayer dollars and related funds. SIGAR works to provide accurate and balanced information, evaluations, analysis, and recommendations to help the U.S. Congress, U.S. agencies, and other decision-makers to make informed oversight, policy, and funding decisions to: |

- improve effectiveness of the overall reconstruction strategy and its component programs;
- improve management and accountability over funds administered by U.S. and Afghan agencies and their contractors;
- improve contracting and contract management processes;
- prevent fraud, waste, and abuse; and
- advance U.S. interests in reconstructing Afghanistan.

| Obtaining Copies of SIGAR Reports and Testimonies | To obtain copies of SIGAR documents at no cost, go to SIGAR's Web site (www.sigar.mil). SIGAR posts all publically released reports, testimonies, and correspondence on its Web site. |

| To Report Fraud, Waste, and Abuse in Afghanistan Reconstruction Programs | To help prevent fraud, waste, and abuse by reporting allegations of fraud, waste, abuse, mismanagement, and reprisal, contact SIGAR's hotline: |

- Web: www.sigar.mil/fraud
- Email: sigar.pentagon.inv.mbx.hotline@mail.mil
- Phone Afghanistan: +93 (0) 700-10-7300
- Phone DSN Afghanistan: 318-237-3912 ext. 7303
- Phone International: +1-866-329-8893
- Phone DSN International: 312-664-0378
- U.S. fax: +1-703-601-4065

| Public Affairs | Public Affairs Officer |

- Phone: 703-545-5974
- Email: sigar.pentagon.ccr.mbx.public-affairs@mail.mil
- Mail: SIGAR Public Affairs
2530 Crystal Drive
Arlington, VA 22202

www.ingramcontent.com/pod-product-compliance
Lightning Source LLC
Chambersburg PA
CBHW081811280526
45789CB00008B/3090